This Bed Our Bodies Shaped

THIS BED
OUR BODIES
SHAPED

POEMS BY

April Lindner

ABLE MUSE PRESS

Able Muse Press

www.ablemusepress.com

Printed in the United States of America

Library of Congress Control Number: 2012933923

ISBN 978-0-9878705-9-9

Cover image: *Welcome To* by Alyssa Monks, © Alyssa Monks

Cover & book design by Alexander Pepple

Able Muse Press is an imprint of *Able Muse: A Review of Poetry, Prose & Art*—at www.ablemuse.com

Able Muse Press
467 Saratoga Avenue #602
San Jose, CA 95129

Acknowledgments

The following journals, anthologies and websites first published these poems, some in slightly different forms or with different titles:

Able Muse: "Our Lady of Perpetual Help."

Apple Valley Review: "Dream House."

Carolina Quarterly: "Baboosic Lake."

Cave Wall: "Waiting."

Crazyhorse: "Eden Estates."

Drexel Online Journal: "Habit."

First Things: "Charmed."

The Formalist: "The Neighbors."

The Fox Chase Review: "Tempted."

Harpur Palate: "Lobsters in the Attic."

The Hudson Review: "Three at Low Tide," "Alchemy," "Widow's Walk," "Trifocals," "Carried Away."

Iron Horse Literary Review: "Dinner at Brigham's."

Loch Raven Review: "The Smell of Men," "The Trip to Brooklyn Misremembered as a Roller Coaster Ride."

Love Poems and Other Messages for Bruce Springsteen: "One-night Stand."

Measure: "Eleven," "Memento," "Backyard Grave," "I Give You Ben," "She," "The Change."

Mezzo Cammin: "Life Study," "Presents for Girls."

MiPoesias: "A Flash, a Lightning Bolt, a Random Blip."

One Trick Pony: "Sweeping Up Shards," "Birthmark."

Poets.org: "Postcard from Rockport."

Prairie Schooner: "Dog Bite," "Nameless," "Starting Over."

The Raintown Review: "Old Guitar."

River Styx: "Red Dress."

The Same: "Dressing for Work."

Sewanee Theological Review: "Kimono."

Washington Square: "Giving Birth on the 37ᵗʰ Floor."

Special thanks to Alex Pepple and Able Muse Press, and to the friends and mentors who read early versions of these poems and provided vital feedback: Melissa Goldthwaite, Tenaya Darlington, Ann Green, Ted Fristrom, Rich Fusco, Jo Alyson Parker, Tom Brennan, Richard Haslam, Mark Jarman, Lynn Levin, Lisa Barnett, Lisa Sewell, David Floyd, Harriet Levin, Terese Parisi, Arlene Humphry, and, last but decidedly not least, the awe-inspiring poets at *Eratosphere*. I am grateful to Marilyn Nelson and Soul Mountain Retreat for the lovely and productive time I spent there. Thanks also to Benjamin Thoele for the use of his haiku, in its entirety, within the poem "I Give You Ben." Belated gratitude to two wonderful teachers, Jean Valentine and Nancy Kenworthy, and to Dana Gioia for being the mentor and friend every writer should be lucky enough to have.

Contents

III

for André

This Bed Our Bodies Shaped

I

Dressing for Work

Mornings he puts on
an air of distraction, his face
clean shaven, its angles sharp,
cuffs buttoned at the wrists,
two slaps of aftershave,
puts on his best, his most
careful self, running lines
before the mirror, eyes opaque
with lists—stops to make,
clients to convince—readies
the act he saves for those
he can't quite trust.
Even his light kiss speaks
of distance, the far compartment
where his day transpires,
its banks of glass overlooking
other offices, its forced air
and florescence, long halls
where he moves among strangers
he works hard to charm.
If asked, he'd say, *Of course*
I'd rather stay with you,
and mean it. Still, she knows—
from the line of his chin,
his long back slanted
toward the door, the new shine

on his good shoes—it's not so,
knows when she phones him
she'll hear a small pause
as he reassembles her
from memory, her features
gathering like mist,
warm breath on a window,
small cloud he'll soon need
to wipe out of the way.

Mid-March

Lost things resurface
waterlogged: one ballet slipper,
a marbled notebook,
its covers stiff, curled back
like wings, and one dead cat—
gray tiger—stretched against the curb . . .
but who could look for long?

This point: the year's pivot,
its rusty hinge, moment to glance back
and shudder at winter,
to look ahead in suspense
toward the buoyant earth
tarted up in bridal finery—
sheer expense of blossom.

But true spring's at least
one freak blizzard off.
Today we're soft, tomorrow
seized by ice. Careful
not to hope, we limp along
on earth churned up, then frozen.

Waiting

Someone's carried off the aquarium,
that burbling, almost breathing box,
from the waiting room where silent women
flip through magazines. I'd have chosen
the seat beside the small warmth
of its lamp, its sapphire lappings.
Fish would flitter up to gulp and gape,
to mouth their ohs before startling back
in infinite loops. Now as I wait
for my name, for a room
and a paper dress, for news
good or bad, I miss their flickering
silvers, blacks, and oranges,
their neon stripes, their fins
that trailed like scarves, shuddered
like flames, how they took
the four glass walls, the pretense
of coral and green pulsing weeds,
as their benevolent planet. What became
of the mollies, the gourami, the tetras,
the blue damselfish? Did they die off
one by one, too much trouble
to replace? I think of them floating
dull-eyed to the surface, scooped and flushed
by the receptionist, brisk in her rounds,
watering the ficus, straightening
the paintings of tulips, her footsteps
swallowed by thick mauve pile.

Nameless

One month the blood came in waves
with pains like labor to double her up,
some mouth in her belly gulping shut
and open. She'd given birth before
and recognized the amniotic scent:
flowers and rust. She hadn't known
of this embryo her body was expelling
and would have screamed to realize it spinning
from her flesh, leaching her bones for bone.
She wouldn't want to live again inside
those breasts like bull's-eyes, belly like a Big Top.
Or to feel the baby's head, a wrecking ball
tearing though plaster. Or to love from scratch
and listen in sleep for breath's absence.
Instead she'll listen many nights
to the stubborn drumming in her ears,
and when her husband reaches for her breast,
her breath will catch, then rush, then catch.
She'll part her legs and some small wish—
unnamed, unnameable, will drift
and batter like a moth against a transom.

Three at Low Tide

I

After rain, he hunches in his anorak
to sweep the beach, run his buzzing disk
across the softened sand. His outstretched wand
jitters like a dowser's or a blind man's,
listens through the crust, sends back
now and then the thrilling whine that signals
some ordinary thing made strange by burial.

II

I sift the sand for bits of glass
dragged out deep then hurled ashore,
in a relentless spiral, useful things

lost overboard or tossed, then rubbed
between the ocean's restless fingers
into these chips, these greens and ambers,

these aquamarines, pinks and teals.
How many months or years of tumbling
soothed their treacherous edges,

suffused their clarity with cloud?
Shot through with cracks and bubbles,
each tablet's inscribed with its small history:

how, earth first, each passed through fire
and into human hands, then plunged
through the water that will hasten it

back into sand. Arrested for a moment
in its trip from stone to vessel
to weapon to totem of sea and time

and, once I release it, to pebble again,
it rests in air, and distills daylight
like fog gone brittle and shattered into bits.

III

More tease than strip, the surf slips back
and though the show runs twice a day
we're fascinated by the slow
disrobing. Shallows webbed with gold
ripple, then draw back to expose
crinkles tender as the lines a bedsheet
etches on skin. Our hands itch
for all they might gather, periwinkles clustered
on wet underledges, the rich nether tangle
of rockweed and knotted wrack.
What's left veiled undulates somewhere,
barracuda, moray, hammerhead,
caressed by the same waves that lap our ankles.
At nightfall, the tide unfurls,
black and glistening, tipped with moon,
to gather all its secrets up in silk.

Tempted

The cyclone fence beside the tracks
tingles; a slight shimmer just beneath notice
gathering until the silvery links thrill
to magnify the news:
                                    an express train
tears through the station, its sirocco
of weight, speed and grit
blasting back the ones who wait,
newspapers folded, coffee gone cold.
I feel beneath the locomotive blowback
a subtle undertow.
                                    The nerves
vibrate like high-pitched strings
strummed awake, the blood surges as if
I've been waiting not for the 8:15
inbound local making all stops

but for this sheer adrenaline spurt
that tempts me into a moment's belief
I might plunge headfirst into that torrent
of steel thrashing steel, into consummation,
a pin summoned by an electromagnet

but it passes. I'm still
upright on this trembling
platform, having passed the test,
having made the sensible choice
not to leap into the thundering gale,
not to embrace the awakening third rail.

One-night Stand

The crowd drifts lightly into the arena,
sifting through the stands, the harsh cement
and worn seats slowly softening with flesh,
till what was still and stony as a canyon
begins to murmur, vibrate. Roadies swarm
the stage, unwinding cables, setting out
a gleaming sax, a battered Fender Esquire.
Each item rates a scattered cheer. Technicians
dangle in the rafters, poised to spill
light from big black buckets. Someone taps
a mike, then strums a chord, a flash of noise
to flood the room and shock the slouchers upright.
When finally the lights flick out, a gasp
precedes the roar of twenty thousand voices
like waves that rasp across a pebbled beach.
The drummer slips onstage; then one by one,
the rest, gilded by footlights, take their stations.
The front man straps on his guitar, counts off:
A-one, a-two, a-one two three four. Fists—
twenty thousand of them—pump in unison.
The pulsing crowd, like an anemone,
waves its grabby filaments, convulsing
toward its maw, the spotlit center where
the singer, dressed in denim, silver chains
and sweat, bends slightly at the knees and stomps
one boot, leans back to wrench the lyrics out.
The congregation screams along by heart,
each straining to be heard, some shrieking out

the names of hits. Forbidden cameras flash.
Those swaying closest to the stage can feel
the bass pulse through their chests, a second heartbeat,
and pressure at their backs, barely restrained,
the crush to meet his eyes, to touch his leg,
to brush his strings or catch one of his picks.
To hear the favorite song they've waited for,
that one about unslakable desire.
This is their moment. Now it's slipping past
too fast, his every move—a windmilled arm,
a long slide on his knees, a mic-stand twirl—
a prophecy, his every phrase a cue
to toss their love into the swelling tide.
And when he yells goodnight and disappears,
they flail their cell phones, blue electric squares
dancing in the dark like tattered rags
waved by the shipwrecked at an empty sky.

Talk Radio

The voices fill her quiet rooms, diction
smooth as tumbled stones, the practiced
lack of accent, soundtrack to her hours.
Weather seems kinder in the abstract, and traffic
seen from the sky is a spill of necklaces,
the litany of clogged routes
a local poetry. The news—always bad,
lately worse—arrives with padded corners;
euphemisms bloom
into the onrush of disaster. It soothes her—
the utter absence of alarm—
no outrage so outrageous
it can't be cauterized. If one story
makes her cry or fume, the next
sweeps it off with dispatch.
Lately she even listens in her sleep
letting the gentle patter furl
her mind's many frazzled threads
onto a single spool. One anchor
narrates the entire world, his words
riding waves that sweep
benignly through her. He whispers
sweet everythings into her earbuds,
escorting her past nightmares into daylight.

She

She knots the dynamite close to her breast
and zips a coat too heavy for the heat
despite the throbbing at her wrists and throat.
I want to know her better. What distress
cools the molten lava into stone,
despair into resolve? Step after step
she bears her body forward to its death
in certainty: somebody must atone.
On the bus, a boy behind her tries
a new route home. It's Wednesday. Who can stay
alert to threat each ordinary day,
interrogate each passing stranger's eyes?
Igneous, she'll shatter but not bend.
What could he say to stay her moving hand?

I Give You Ben

White-blonde and earnest, on an Air Force scholarship,
premed poet, slow to raise his hand.
Ben with his haiku: *A slice of white bread/*
peanut butter and jelly/a slice of white bread,
who stopped by uniformed to say goodbye,
incongruous beneath his stiff blue cap,
before they shipped him out. Today I see
the ROTCs running laps, their wiry frames,
and lambent smiles against the crimson track,
and feel, against my will, a tug of gratitude.
When they're gone to pitch tents in the desert
awaiting orders, or to the crumbling streets
of Baghdad where they'll see the startled faces
of those they'll have to kill—a freshman crop
will spring up straight as corn. In what exchange—
my pleasant house, the bedrooms, gently lit,
in which my young sons sleep, guarded by pets—
I wonder, would I choose to give you Ben—
as if he were a coin, and mine to give.

for Ben Thoele

18

Old Guitar

It leaned, outgrown, two decades in the attic:
six sclerotic strings, the neck arched back
in what looked like pain. To hold it now—
polished and restrung—feels almost wayward
like returning to a former boyfriend,
his heft, his sun-warmed back, those very freckles
I'd struggled to forget. It wants to float,
hollow in my hands, the wafery wood
smooth against my palm, the body curved
to fit my own. Its surface glows like sun
through honey, and the tight-coiled nickel strings
store an almost-hum of energy.
I stretch to eke a G chord out, then strike
a deadwood D. No, I was never good,
impatient and distracted by my heroes—
their amplifier towers and whammy bars,
nimble hands I'd watch for hours, imagining
the range of touch from gentle to emphatic.
I strum again and each note jangles up
against the next, vibrations magnified
almost into music. Fingerboard
and rosewood bridge, the shiny tuning pegs,
the hole like an eclipse: it wants me back.
An old progression rises up from memory,
gone soft, my fingers burn, but I press harder
until an A chord chimes out and sustains.

Wuthering Heights

An airless attic for our first apartment,
we slept all summer on the floor, a fan
lurching back and forth to shunt hot wind
across our skin. Sheet wrapped around your head,

naked ankles poking out, your arm
an oak limb felled across my back, you slept
through brawls and bottles breaking on the streets
we didn't dare to walk through after dark.

Days, our landlord and his drunken cousin
hammered at the bathtub pipes. I'd turn
the oven on and roaches would stream out
in waves across the burners. I was reading,

for the seventh time, *Wuthering Heights.*
Heathcliff bashed his skull against a trunk,
Cathy died in childbirth, her cold ghost
begging at the window—*let me in*—

her wrist sawed bloody on the shattered pane.
In the other room, you stayed up late,
stretching canvas after canvas, painting
smokestacks, iron girders, twisted bridges,

a factory worker fallen, arms flung wide
like Jesus on the cross, a sun-bleached street
through which a woman with my face danced naked,
and smashed our wedding dishes. But some nights

you'd feel your way back through the dark to find me
sleeping, lift the damp and twisted sheets
and brush my stomach with your fingertips,
then with your hair. You smelled of linseed oil

—your medium—and turpentine—your solvent.
Like the earth in rain, I'd soften, opening
to drink you in, your touch my slumber's solvent,
our medium the dark. Those early days

a source of little visible delight
but necessary, like the rocks beneath.

The Neighbors

Our houses stand like lovers, hip to hip,
the only thing between, a grassy strip,

the fence an empty gesture, but we know
them only well enough to say hello.

Their pear tree dumps its produce in our yard,
mealy and bewormed, or green and hard.

Our dogs annoy them, barking to get in,
sniffing between pickets, and the din

when the teenage girl rehearses with her band
reminds me just how middle-aged I am.

The wife drags out the trash and mows the lawn
in her sweatpants, looking put upon.

I've watched the undershirted husband preen
then glance my way, expecting to be seen.

Etiquette demands we all pretend
I'm looking at their lawn gnomes, not at them.

Why do I dislike them? It's complex.
We hear them break their dishes and have sex,

and bite back our own cries of rage and love
out of concern for what they think of us.

Divorce

Stripped bare, the house we coveted
revealed its cracks and creaks. Our footsteps
echoed as we took the solemn walkthrough.
Whose history had we gotten ourselves into?

Pale rectangles where portraits hung,
basement strewn with discards—
gilded picture frames ornately empty,
bones of an old double bed.

In the living room, someone
stained the blond floorboards dark
but stopped halfway, stark demarcation
like an edge someone could plummet from.

They left one room half papered.
Already the edges roll back,
the paste exhausted. But then
there's the garden, planted

to lure monarch and hummingbird.
Over time, we'll learn its ways.
When the last tulip crumples,
irises will spring up, fresh shoots

nudging through from snowmelt
to first frost. Their blended scents
will waft through open windows
every summer we're lucky enough

to live here, a distraction
like perfume to cover up the hint
of some small animal
left dead in the walls.

Charmed

Home from a party
the silver balloon
followed me.
From room to room,

it bumped the ceiling
in my wake
morning to night.
By some freak

of draft or static
electricity—
it waltzed as if charmed.
Why did it choose me,

not my husband
or sons, to chase?
When the helium weakened
it sank to face

level and bobbed,
nodding assent
to my every choice.
Still not content,

for days it stalked
unshakably.
Its ribbon hung down,
synecdoche

suggesting a torso
pathetic and spare.
I'd turn and confront my
reflected stare.

As it grew wrinkled
it followed still
rubbing against me
at ankle height till,

annoyed, I tied it
to a chair's back.
In a distant corner
it dangles, slack,

a slighted suitor
or castoff pet.
I should throw it out
but haven't yet.

Starting Over

Blossoms swell and brush my window,
heavy with sap, and red at the center.
I can't say what kind. Next door,
my neighbor kneels in shallow soil
where roses mingle with spinach.
He refuses at first to tell me his name,
insists I couldn't pronounce it.
He welcomes me to Ohio with rhubarb
and stories of his childhood village
where boys toss dynamite in the river,
and swim to gather the floating fish,
where women wear robes of cobweb,
and soften their skin with turmeric lotion.
Where friends who pass on the street
bow to honor the spark of god
in each other's eyes. *And you*, he asks,
what brings you so far from your home?
When I reply, he *tsks*, and hands me
a bouquet of veined, vermilion chard.
Does he still dream, I wonder,
in his native tongue? He bends
to root up onions for my supper,
rehearsing their name in his language:
Oolyee, oolyee. Like waves on a shore.

Dream House

What if this house were every house
we'd inhabited, lost friends
to startle us from the doorway,
each broken dish seamlessly mended,
stacked in a limitless cupboard?
All the pets we buried
bumping our ankles, nudging to be fed?
What if this house were every house
we'd longed to live in? My cottage,
shingles weathered a Cape Cod gray,
your cabin just below the treeline.
All that transpired as planned and all
that surprised us? Paintings
you imagined against closed lids.
Babies we left unconceived,
burbling, squalling, suffering first teeth.
Our daughter as we dreamed her,
on the lawn blowing bubbles,
sleek as an otter, nose
sunburnt, as glad to see us
as if we'd been away.
Would it be a kind of heaven,
a house expanding like a baking loaf,
our acts and our intentions
married and multiplied, a kaleidoscope
of bright, rattling beads and shards
mirrored into crystal symmetry?

II

Giving Birth on the 37th Floor

Obedient, I breathed. The night breathed back,
streetlights pulsing open, shut.

The hard node at my core
softening to crack, the sepals

struggling to spread.
The delicate labellum, stunned petals

curling back, the ruby stigma
naked to the air—the filament,

the tender fuzz—flesh that can tear.
While I waited, the dawn burst purple.

Orange spread like yolk
and swirled, no joy unmixed.

The sun insisted: crimson, garnet, wine,
and my body gasped and ripened and spread wide

to free his weak first cry.

Soon the sky was eggshell white,
an ordinary day, bearing no trace,

but over every door a light still burned.

Dinner at Brigham's

Never mind the cold rain,
trees soaked and heavy,
pavement streaked by stoplights;

in Brigham's glowing storefront, radiators
thunked with warmth. A bell tinkled
whenever the door opened onto twilight,

letting wind sweep in. Each Wednesday,
the doctor let me listen to your heartbeat—
rush of surf I had to tell myself was you.

Then I'd pretend at my usual table
to read the paper till the teenage waitress—
the bored tilt of her shoulder,

her wispy hair yanked back—became
a picture I can call back ten years later.
That night I'd meet your father at Lamaze,

and lean back in his arms, as if each deep,
theatrical breath could steel me
for the amniotic tide, the blood and grunting,

the pain of stretching wide to launch a planet,
trials to which I might well be unequal.
But those peaceful, ordinary meals

afloat in the pink womb of Brigham's,
still seem a sacred time, when things
I know now were still mysterious—

the cheerful, impossible, perpetual noise,
and how when you go out to school or play,
the bare floors ring with silence—

when alone, but not, I held my glass of milk,
measured each sip and every breath,
as cell by cell, the thought of you grew flesh.

Birthmark

I find it by touch,
the skin raised and furred,
brown splotch on his thigh
like all the body's shadows
gathered to a single spot.
When they gave him, newborn,
into my arms, I noticed it first—
before his old man's eyes,
his grasping fingers,
the loose parchment skin
over not enough flesh—
like something I'd done wrong,
a stain I could go back
and paint over. There are ways:
scalpels and lasers and scopes
for cutting out any trace
of what pools and threatens to spread.
I'll try not to think how that sly mark
punctuates his knee, how I'll forget
and look for what I look for first:
coin borne like gold on an Argive's eyes
from one world to the next.

Lobsters in the Attic

He won't eat corn till I remove the *risk,*
his word for silk, won't eat the kernels touched
by *risk,* though corn is mostly safe, familiar.
For him, most food *is* risky: squishy, weird,
spicy, touched by bugs, and when he asks,
Why are so many lobsters in the attic?
he means earwigs. Through his wary eyes,
a lobster's just a monster arthropod,
its creamy flesh offset by those antennae,
and the green *tamale* I pretend to like,
(the liver, slick and rich, a luxury).
What passes his inspection? Purple jelly,
yellow cheese, candy in any hue.
Surely not this basket of mulberries,
freshly picked. I wash, searching for inchworms
(find one rearing up, green question mark),
look closely at the berry's clustered bumps
like rampant cells. I have to force myself
to eat a single one, its burst peculiar
on my tongue. We learn to chew,
mouths closed, the laundered napkins on our laps,
learn to overlook the strings and bruises,
the nerves and messy juice, and say *delicious.*

Dog Bite

The worst for him was his friend turned wolf,
and the blood that splattered as he ran. The worst
for us: the hospital, his upper lip tugged back
to show the gash—the flesh halved deeply,
cleanly—while I hold him for the needle
that rubs pain out. He submits
to the quick stitch, the thread black
against pink skin, calm now he sees
the doctor can be trusted, his voice
soothing, his face clean shaven,
the clues that signal kindness to a child.
He's worried, though, about his pet
who *didn't mean it, Mom.* His voice is flat.
He knows the months he's tried to woo this dog
were over when it leapt for his throat
and caught his mouth. The scars, at least,
will be invisible. At home, he'll sleep,
big boy between his parents, till he's sure
no beast will tear into his dreams. And we
will want him there, our bodies makeshift walls.
We who led the stranger to our home,
fixed him a bowl, taught him to sleep
under our blankets, we who taught our son
to rub the muzzle that sheathes the teeth.

Carried Away

One rainy night we sat in traffic
and, overtired in back, you saw
a wind-whipped grocery bag afloat
beyond the clutch of jagged branches,
swept by gusts and whirled in eddies.
A sudden downdraft swooped it earthward,
where it danced till with a whoosh
a current luffed it past the powerlines.
Disowned by gravity, small ghost
not yet snagged by twiggy fingers,
it couldn't reach the earth. Thin-skinned,
it pulsed, translucent jellyfish.
You wept and pled to be let out
into the dark and slanted rain,
to somehow save that desolate thing.
The light turned green and still you begged,
Go back, go back, on its behalf,
caught and held, bossed and tossed
by a will much greater than its own.

Backyard Grave

With two lines from Bruce Springsteen

Everything dies, baby, that's a fact.
I dig a backyard grave while he stands by.
But maybe everything that dies someday comes back

to life? He cups his fish. I try for tact.
To make room for new minnows, old ones die.
Everything dies, baby. That's a fact.

I show him how the soil turns rich and black
from crumbled leaves and bark, so in a way
maybe everything that dies someday comes back,

but not itself. This notion stings, a smack
unearned and unprepared for. *Tell me why*
everything dies. Baby, that's a fact

I'd alter if I could. Heaven's no help—
ethery and cold, blank as the sky.
But maybe everything that dies someday comes back

a turtle or an elephant? One speck
of comfort, maybe not an outright lie:
Everything dies, baby, that's a fact,
but maybe everything that dies someday comes back.

Eleven

His scowls announce the change about to come:
he shrinks from hugs. Already, he's begun—
his frame still delicate, his skin like cream,
his freckled chin, his feet the size of mine—
new, scary calculations: *If I say*
NO and don't back down, what can she do?
He practices degrees of cool disdain
and searing rage. Then—sometimes—peeking through,
our gentle son comes back to share a meal
or tell a joke, himself, but tentative.
I love you, Mom, now sounds like an appeal
for future misdemeanors. It's let him live
awhile, the force that pinned him in its grip,
a bored housecat that lets its plaything slip.

Hypophysis

Hard as a nut, the brain's small knot
knows before we do it's time
for the bud to crack,
its liquid cache exposed
to air and any wayward buzz.

I know what to tell the daughter
I don't have, but to my son,
more bee than bloom, swept everywhere
by a malicious wind,
                    what should I say?

His wings beat in the gust
that blows him out of reach,
and the word that escapes my lips,
no help, no help at all, is *stay*.

Baboosic Lake

My mother would row us out—
the sky streaked with fresh blood,
the black flies biting hard.
Trout would gain the air, flop back
as if yanked. She'd bait her hook.
Balanced on the center plank
I bore once more the stillness,
the far-off radio distorted to a moan.
I held my breath as we approached the bend
around which we might find anything
but found more of the same. One mountain,
Monadanock, rose in the distance, purple
and past my grasp. Mother would reel her fish,
hold it aloft, its whole body a clenched muscle.
I wonder what she hoped to hear me say
and why I had to freight my praise
with boredom and disdain. Forever
she would cast her line and wait,
and I would trail one hand in water soft as oil,
my wavering white fingers drawing a crowd,
small fish staring till one darted up
to take that first exploratory nibble.

Habit

When at thirteen the flesh began
its mutiny of swelling hips,
of errant blood and rampant hair,
I looked deliberately away,
my gaze fixed on a book, my shoes,
the frog split wide, pinned to the desk.
I traced its oviducts and spleen
while what was straight and without fuss,
what smelled of bread and healthy sweat,
grew startlingly ornate, a riot
of grabby tendrils and sticky blooms.
One day I'd weigh my breasts in hand,
admit they might not be so bad.
One day I'd walk a hushed *musée*
past a gold-trimmed, child-sized robe
and think how stiff the wimple, how heavy
the cross she wore around her neck.
But first I had to dress in darkness,
layer over layer, cringing
from mirror, fingertips and mother,
her tape measure and mouth of pins.
How good a habit would have been,
generous and dun, a gown
to hide the body so, ignored,
it might swing freely, like a bell.

Stairway to Heaven

Dim lights plus music equaled
charmed invisibility: a boy's hands dug
into a girl's back pockets; a girl,
eyes shut, bore her partner's weight.
Humid perfume rose like steam
to fill the gym. A boy hovered,
eager for an unclaimed girl to press against.
I didn't know his name, but when his tongue,
slick with nicotine and mint, wormed past my teeth,
I swayed till the slow song died
and found a crowd of girls to hide in.
How, I wondered, would I learn to like it?
I mouthed the lyrics of the last-chance slow dance.
Nobody told how the first ripples
would stutter in stop motion like poured water
broken by strobe light into drops,
each clumsy tumble
launching a slow corona,
to stir me at last and spread rings.

The Smell of Men

A mix of mildew, hops, fermenting yeast.
A dark brown sourdough pungency. The first
time I noticed, I was cutting through
the dormitory boy's wing, underground,
sunless and a little dank. The furnace

hum, the exit sign's electric whine,
the slivered light beneath each bedroom door,
were seasoned with the humid musk that rose
from rumpled sheets, the sticky mist of showers,
the captive breath, the sweat and Ivory soap

and pheromones of sixteen boys-slash-men.
A virgin then, I paused to draw that air
into my lungs, to memorize its taste
before I passed into the crisp blue morning.
We had, back then, a law no one enforced:

no girls allowed in boys' rooms after midnight.
It wasn't long until I found myself
sneaking from a boy's cracked door at dawn—
my hair unruly, teeth unbrushed, in clothes
I'd shed the night before—through that same wing,

and gingerly upstairs, the floorboards squealing,
it seemed, under my weight, hoping no hall mate
would catch me stealing back into my room.
Before too many nights, the smell of men
had seeped into my pores, an air I wore

like Shalimar, a veil of it between
my skin and blouse, so heady I would sniff
my wrist and tremble. Could the other girls
detect it? And—more thrillingly—the boys?
With time I grew accustomed to the scent.

I'd wander through that long hallway of men,
breathing deeply, trying to discern
that burnished note that once had signaled sex,
a landlocked girl's first breath of ocean air,
the briny wind that tingles like a slap.

Life Study

The screen, as if to view me were forbidden.
The robe, rubbed thin by bodies it has hidden.

The plywood platform costumed in a sheet
adorned with bottles and a sheaf of wheat.

The half-lit room, its easels in two rows,
each with a stranger waiting for the pose.

My hands like dead weight dangling at each side.
Though I might wish for one, no place to hide.

My hope: to be a shape in air, a gesture,
to meet nobody's eyes while the professor

moves me into place. His studied hand
which tugs my arm and shows me how to stand.

The spotlight flooding half my flesh with heat.
My other side in shadow. My cold feet.

And at the break, their sketches on display,
each with a different angle to convey,

sum up the profile, belly, hips and thighs
of somebody I barely recognize.

Presents for Girls

Identical, the gifts our parents brought:
twin baby dolls or bunnies, or we'd whine
and fight over who got the blonder doll,
the blue rabbit and not its yellow sibling.
We drooled for stuff that makes me wince these days:
the girly-pink aisle of the Toys"R"Us:
the dream mansions and Cinderella castles,
the sacred Barbie bridal gown and Ken
slick in his satin tux. White go-go boots,
ballerina slippers, and the purses:
white for Easter with a tidy clasp
and empty spaces we would someday fill
with matchbooks, wallets and mascara wands—
grownup goods withheld and marveled over—
the credit cards and magic butane lighter,
the fragile, pale and glamorous cigarette,
the breath mints and the ticket stubs. How alien
to be a woman in sharp heels, how powerful
that aura of Chanel. To have a baby,
not a baby doll, to have a husband
handsome as the Prince from *Sleeping Beauty*—
clean shaven in a uniform. To drive a car
and go out in the night in rhinestone earrings
and not be left in rose-dotted pajamas
on Grandma's couch to squabble over popcorn,
with pocketbooks we'd click open and shut
waiting for a token to appear there
of the lives we'd been rehearsing for.

Widow's Walk

The locals know to call it Marble*head*.
(I hungered then to call myself a local.)
I see you there, you claimed, and drove me East
to glimpse the crooked lighthouse and the harbor,
the moonwhite sloops whose moorings tinked like bracelets.
The narrow streets snaked uphill between houses
crowding like tourists, vying for a view,
each crowned with a widow's walk, its handrails
scrolled like iron script. I ached to pace,
to wring my hands, a pale, Victorian bride
defying lightning, glamorous with grief.
And in your narrow bed, my limbs still riding
the rise and fall of waves, my skin still burnt
by the wind that sweeps the causeway, crisp as gin,
I dreamed a ship by night, its distant lantern
rounding the horizon, dreamed I'd found
a way to stay, a way to make you love me.

Red Dress

That night I dressed slowly—
red dress, black heels,
lacy white ankle socks,
mascara, lipgloss, *Magie Noire.*
Not wanting to look eager,
I stopped to kill ten minutes
at a store between razed cornfields.
Behind the register, a skinny kid
barely looked up as I wandered
past bundled newspapers, dusty cans.
The door jangled and in swept
two burly, bowlegged men
in dusty jeans and greasy hair.
They sauntered through the store,
not pausing, not planning to buy.
My dread summoned them,
blood tracked in the forest.
One hitched his thumb
in my direction. *Hey, Chuck,
check this out.* They snickered,
took a step forward. I stepped back.
They leaned in, breathing
tobacco, mint and whiskey.
Loosen up, bitch, said Chuck.
I spun and wobbled
to a dim booth at the back,

clung to the receiver, punched
random numbers. They blocked
my way out while I babbled
to the dial tone . . . *yes, well,*
I should be home soon.
Look out for me. They watched
till, running out of fake chat,
grasping, I held one hand
over the receiver to ask,
Can I help you? They laughed,
leaned on one another,
staggered off, snorting.
I clutched the phone a long time,
emerged on shaky legs. Steadied
my hands on the steering wheel.
Floored it. In my new boyfriend's
cinderblock apartment, I tried
to make my panic convincing.
He asked, *What did you think?*
They would rape you right there
in the store? and poured more wine.
You need to chill out, babe.
But he liked my dress, approved
of the anklets a schoolgirl
might wear, the teetering heels
in which it would have been
impossible to run.

A Flash, a Lightning Bolt, a Random Blip

I feel my being dance from ear to ear
– Theodore Roethke

One moment I'm staring into my teacup
at a shifting milky cloud and the next

a narrow alley opens into light:

the sunswept stone of St. Mark's Square—
tourists, pigeons, vendors at their stalls,
and just beyond, the pale green Adriatic.
Vaporetti buzz past, churn up mist.

I was here once: my body remembers.

My knees bend to deliver me
into the crowd. My scalp recalls
that day's heat, and my nostrils
fill again with honeydew and ancient, bookish dust.
Or I'm swaying on the Tobin Bridge,
trucks thrumming on all sides, and sunrise
smouldering in the windows of North Boston,

or, still more distant, a kitchen,
the harvest gold Frigidaire humming.

My legs dangle from the high stool—

Am I four? Six? The air is brown
with London broil and roast potatoes.
The kitchen timer softly ticks
and for a moment, I'm as present, there,

as ever, this vision, like the others,
brief and vivid as a flashbulb's pop.
This trick of memory, this little gift—
is it the coffee? A random pattern
of sunlight on tile? Or nothing more
than a misfired serotonin jolt, that launches me
as if the past were someplace I could visit,

as if there could be such a thing as "past,"

when even the present sizzles from synapse to synapse:
blinding, ordinary, gorgeous, gone.

III

Alchemy

When the tide retracts
it leaves a delicate line
of sodium and rust.

Slick wisps, feathers and tendrils,
the usual trashed shells.

A man-of-war pulsates,
clear and venomous, transplanted heart.

A stranger passing through this landscape,
I linger, wanting the currents of sea and air

to smooth me into purity
like seaglass battered edgeless,

the way the ocean rinses the exhausted air.

Here trees twist sideways,
blasted, grasping for stasis,
dunes smoothed and ridged,

things shaped by motion
or shapeless because they themselves
are motion: the churning that is the sea,

the chuffing we call wind,

the fins that razor forward
through shifting minnow clouds
and overhead, one silver jet

a needle shirring the distance.

Bedford Stuyvesant

I'd heard it spoken of with awe—
poorer than the South Bronx, bloodier
than the Meat Packing District—and here I was,
one wrong turn hurtling my car straight into its heart.

If I locked my doors, expecting Crips and Bloods,
what I found was an odd hush at midday,
streets so broken the dirt bloomed through,
whole lots rippling with chest-high grass,

trees spreading wide, fringed leaves
through second-story windows. Smashed glass
glinted on each narrow thoroughfare,
and children played, careless of traffic and strangers.

One was barefoot in a windfall
of broken bottles. If I could describe
his eyes, his upraised arms, his thin calves
laced with scratches, if I could coax

a bud that waits unnoticed in the rubble
to crack open and reveal its ruby core, vibrant
as any hothouse flower, and if I made you see
its tender freckles, its filaments,

you could turn the page feeling absolved,
and I could forget how I fumbled for my map,
so clearly a trespasser and lost,
so sure each face would mark my presence.

Instead my car left no shadow, as silent
as the streets themselves, as if
I could step out, unnoticed,
and walk like a white ghost through the streets.

As if I could touch that barefoot child,
his skin powdered with dust,
and my hand would pass
like warmth through his delicate chest.

Our Lady of Perpetual Help

The burnt church up the street yawns to the sky,
its empty windows edged in soot, its portals
boarded up and slathered with graffiti,
oily layers, urgent but illegible.
All that can be plundered has been, all
but the carapace—the hollow bell tower,
the fieldstone box that once served as a nave.
The tidy row of homes that line this block
have tended lawns and scalloped bathtub shrines.
Each front porch holds a chair where no one sits.
Those who live here triple lock their doors
day and night. Some mornings they step out
to find a smoking car stripped to its skeleton
abandoned at the curb. Most afternoons
the street is still but for a mourning dove
and gangs of pigeons picking through the grass.
Our Lady of Perpetual Help is gray,
a dead incisor in a wary smile.
A crevice in her wall allows a glimpse
into the chancel, where a sodden mattress
and dirty blanket indicate that someone
finds this place a sanctuary still,
takes his rest here, held and held apart
from passersby, their cruelties and their kindnesses,
watched over by the night's blind congregation,
by the blank eyes of a concrete saint.

Tuesdays at the Art Museum

On Mondays the museum locks its doors
to sleep the weekend rush off. Tuesday mornings
have a starting-over feel: a man
in coveralls rides a hydraulic lift

to change a bulb, observed by painted burghers;
guards in doorways rocking on their heels
stand aside to let me through; curators
prowl the hallways clutching pens and clipboards.

Tiny sounds are magnified, my heels
against parquet, the microclimate meter's
fussy click, the whispering of children
lined up for a lecture on Van Eyck.

Suits of armor brandishing their halberds
form a gauntlet, slight as girls but poised
to slaughter. Adorations and assumptions,
tapestries, their allegories worn

and bleached to beige, small treasures set on velvet,
drenched in white-hot light—a copper brooch,
chalices, a gold-encrusted pyx—
ordinary things aglow with mystery.

I find the Gothic doorway and step through
into a ruin-scavenged cloister, fountain
burbling at its heart. Beneath a ceiling
painted gray, I can pretend at vespers,

can summon something almost like belief
till voices chase me off. Poached from a tomb,
a knight lies in perpetual state, his nose
chunked off, his shield as pockmarked as the moon.

Behind him runs a wall of *Maestàs,*
the sidelong stares of saints and donors sized
by rank, poised in their golden bubbles. Gilt
flattens out the empty space between them.

The painters' care is patterning, not portraiture,
the play of light on silk, smooth faces stacked
in pyramids like produce on display.
The galleries are filling now. I hurry

forward through the centuries to see
the thing I've missed, the human face in three
dimensions—flawed like any in this room,
impatient, haughty, curious, contrite—

emerging from the many-layered darkness.

Self-Portrait as Frida Kahlo

You've seen my face—my black-winged brow,
a raptor swooping for the kill,
flushed cheeks, a grave and tender mouth
and downy upper lip, my piercing
gaze—so many times the shock—
a ribbon wrapped around a bomb—
has lost its charge. Still you've come
where all is held by cool gray walls
to see the canvases my hands
primed and painted, surfaces
I filled with humid life, a sticky
rainforest of vines and orchids,
succulents and strangler figs,
monkeys, dragonflies and parrots,
pampered little hairless dogs.
You've come to see my masquerade,
the lace, the fringe, and peasant blouses,
thorns that knot around my throat,
a hummingbird strung like a charm,
to wonder if I felt its panicked
heart against my own. You've heard
the stories, seen the narrow bed
I painted from, my skeleton
pieced together, braced by metal,
my spine like chalk, my pelvis glued
together like a shattered bowl.

I swam in bright arterial blood,
and drowned in love that battered me
ashore and tugged me out again
and cupped me like a tidepool while
I cooled into a corpse. How could
my story fail to be a part
of what you see here, framed and hung?
Like this *recuerdo* of my friend
falling from her penthouse terrace
to sprawl on concrete in a party
dress, corsage of yellow roses
pinned in place, the broken bones
still strung in place to hold her shape.

St. Theresa in Ecstasy

After Gian Lorenzo Bernini

The angel, when he comes at last
in a trumpet blast of light
glistens like a newborn, smooth
of cheek and chest, his slender waist
cinched in wind-washed gauze. She'd willed
this visit, prayed for days, refusing
sleep and food. Now he appears
beside her, naked arm drawn back.
His fingertips caress a spear,
point it at her heart; his smile
betrays amusement. This could be
the moment just before his arrow
plunges through her breast—*as if
to pierce my very entrails,*
she would write—or it could be
the aftermath. Her heavy vestments
lift and rustle; from their depths
she swoons, lips parted, body curling
upward toward that flame-tipped arrow,
that cauterizing point, and though
the whole tableau is stone, she vibrates
like a harp string as the hand
draws back. One bare foot clings to earth
as, limp, she crests a wave of pain
surpassing sweetness, tasted once
and hungered after: *Now the soul
is satisfied with nothing less.*

Postcard from Rockport

Cold as a slap, this indigo sea,
where we clamber on blonde-fringed rocks,
where someone's tarted up the fishing shacks
with red paint and artful nets.

The sun floats like ice in a highball.
Condos train their plate-glass gazes
on the horizon, amnesiac
to past conspiracies of cloud,

storms that shook homes and swallowed boats.
Just north, a granite wall's etched with the lost—
decades of their half-remembered names.

Imagine waking always to this spread—
each day the ocean swelling
to loll at your feet, exotic pet.

The galleries glow, ripe with impasto,
sunsets we could bite into:
raspberries, marzipan, seafoam like cream.

Their artists shoot for the numinous,
overlook the jagged and impermanent:

barnacles overtaking the dock,
clustered mussels, tangled kelp
and the steady lament
of pebbles tugged senseless from shore.

The Trip to Brooklyn Misremembered
as a Roller Coaster Ride

Lock your doors, they'd say. *Look straight ahead.*
Every other Saturday we'd travel
from Long Island to Grandma's house in Brooklyn,
my parents anxiously accelerating
through neighborhoods they'd gladly left behind.
In the backseat, secretly, we thrilled
with vertigo, craning our necks to gape
at tenements and billboards. We admired
the smashed-out windows and oily graffiti—
so much more satisfying than the misdeeds
we dared dream up. Buckled in the backseat,
we drowsed, secure. But once Dad took a wrong turn
past a cemetery—not the first I'd seen,
but enormous: rows and rows of headstones
in strict formation, interspersed by obelisks
and mausoleums dreadful in their heaviness.
A graveyard gray and scalloped as the ocean
and seemingly as endless, stretching on
for blocks until I couldn't help but know:
the dead were gaining on the living, soon
they would be everywhere. I squinched my eyes
and counted ten but when I peeked we still
were driving past tombstones that grew more ancient,
pale and straight at first, but later crooked,
dark with car exhaust, ground down by age—

the way our grandmother kept growing shorter—
the city underground crowded with bodies
like the one above, each skeleton
waiting in its windowless apartment,
and everyone I'd ever grow to love
would wind up buried here. Our Buick climbed
the ramp onto the Brooklyn-Queens Expressway,
a clackety, steep track. Chains scraped us onward,
grinding toward a peak high as a skyscraper—
a long pause—then the sudden giddy plunge,
the Naugahyde seats falling out beneath us.
We hovered, breathless, bracing for the drop.

Eden Estates

On the narrow porch they sit, and wait, and sit,
in wheelchairs, behind walkers, too many
like goldfish who crowd the surface
for flecks of food. They eye their rectangle
of lawn, the single palm cupped by a sky
so blue it hurts. Sometimes a bicycle
hums past or a car blunders by
blurred with motion they hunger after.

When I drive up, each face tugs mine,
hoping I've come to share hoarded peppermints.
Her face among theirs—
still her face, but sunken and dull—
takes a while to light with recognition.
Happy to see me, she can't stop crying,
her gnarled hand on my arm
softer than it looks, softer than talc.

We head for the beach. She sits at my side
watching the sea like a stage.
I want to hear her stories once more:
how her mother scrubbed floors for money
and left her with the Sisters for safekeeping,
but found a husband and came back
to bring her home. The sun full on her face,
she shuts her eyes and won't speak
of the past, won't pretend any future.

I don't know how to say it's time to leave.
The boardwalk quavers with heat.
In plain flat shoes she must hate,
she's steadier than she looks.
As I drop her off, I bend for a kiss
and she clutches me, strong with longing
to hold me here against goodbye
in this fishbowl of wan and watching faces.

Kimono

Eriko wraps me in her *tomesode,*
so I can feel the heft of ceremony,
the protocol of every tuck and fold.
She hands me one-toed socks, holds me steady
as I pull her sandals on, tells me the names:
Hadajuban, tabi, obi, zōri.
Speech between us sputters like a brook
over jagged rocks, but each crisp gesture
says goodbye precisely. She'll fly home
Tuesday to Sapporo where her mother
wanes in a white bed, circled by nurses.
In Japan—she shapes each word with effort—
we do not tell a person she has cancer.
She guides me first into the inner robe
and then, like a reward, the winged kimono,
a swallowtail of orange, red and gold.
Her deft hands skim the surface, tug a hidden
string in place. *Doesn't your mother guess?*
I think of nausea and blinding pain,
an autumn of black hair. Eriko pauses,
says *maybe.* With a swift, efficient yank,
she tightens the wide sash. In her mirror,
my face bobs on a river of brocade.
She pins my hair in place, smoothing it down,
making order, expert hands attending
to the little rules that tie us to our lives.

Trifocals

Now vision comes in layers, like a cake.
The iced top layer is for movie screens,
help I've needed since the second grade,

since the first pair, powder blue with rhinestones,
cupped my eyes like Siamese fighting fish,
lazy in their bowls. Those glasses changed

how the world saw me—at a remove.
They translated the blackboard's fog to letters,
the smudged horizon into sea or mountains.

The center level's for the middle distance
awkward places just beyond my reach—
the shelves of grocery stores, the vivid boxes

promising their miracles. A buffer
between the near and far, a cushy spot,
the creamy middle, not unlike these years

between uncertainties of youth and age:
lost days of pleasing by my looks alone;
the time when passing strangers will not see me.

The bottom layer magnifies the words
that used to spring forth, ready to be read,
but now withhold their meanings, cryptic runes

to tease my tired eyes. The dry and spongy
bottom of this intricate confection—
the least enticing part. Now that my view

encompasses beginning, middle, end,
there's no forgetting what's around the bend.
I see what's coming closer all too clearly.

The Change

But when did winter fall? Is this November?
The trees I pass each day but rarely notice—
a row of oaks, a birch, two spindly ginkgos—
stand austere and black, singed candlewicks,
the flames of autumn blown out overnight.

All but one: an adolescent maple
balanced on a hill as if in motion,
half clad in trembling gold—the bottom half—
like an awkward girl undressed but for
a billowing skirt, her startled arms defenseless.

I think abruptly of the change of life—
bland euphemism for this very moment—
as from this curb I step into awareness
of half my life blown past, cerise and scarlet
peeling off to wither at my feet.

Not long ago I was that naked girl
the tree resembles, hungry to be seen
but trembling to hide something of herself—
now I must learn to be the one who sees,
transparent as a smoke wisp, unremarkable

to those who hurry, eyes on the horizon.
Soon the maple's branches will wave bare
and she'll resemble, not an ingénue
but something rough-barked, skeletal and stark.
And who will I be? It's not hard to age:

just wait and watch the dark pour in, a moment
earlier each day. It seemed the sultry
afternoons would stretch on endlessly
the pliant earth so lushly strewn with grass,
flimsy blossoms springing from each limb.

Dry

Sensation reaches me
through a layer of felt.
Who swaddled my nerve endings?

My body's a parched garden.
Touched, leaves crumble to dust.
The branches blighted,
the fruit thwarted.

They said it would be so.
I wait for nothing. Want nothing.

Only the sky glows,
brilliant and empty,
a cold celestial blue
in which no bodies touch.

The months run together
without event, a respite
from hunger and blood.

Nothing grows or decays.
I should be thirsty
but I've learned to go without,

can barely remember water's power
to transform, ordinary pebbles
slicked by a retreating wave,
singing against each other in the surf

or an approaching storm,
the fishbowl air gone green and sticky.
And the payoff: rain's sheen
blessing every crevice.

Seen without desire,
the world's edges blur,
its points rubbed blunt.

The wishing well's full
of dusty pennies and
nothing to spend them on.

The Span

How slender it turned out to be,
thin and brilliant as light
that haloes a locked door,
the span between the first urgent
shed rosepetals of blood
and the last, from the moment
the sentence was pronounced
and I wept to be called *woman*
to this release, the shackles sprung,
the strange lightness in my limbs.
Goodbye to months measured by promises
that ripened, trembled and dropped,
each one liquid and distinct,
a pomegranate seed
with its single, hard eye.

Memento

Bad rap for the bones. More permanent
than muscle, hair or blood, they lie alone,
memento mori always. We praise heart,
cuticle and spleen, but say it, *bone,*
and there's the slightest knell, word you intone
rather than pronounce, and in our art
the skull however rendered is a stone
to swallow, stern reminder to be smart,
waste not a moment, taste each grape, repent,
smell the coffee *and* the roses, telephone
your loved ones, think of how your light is spent.
Be in the Now. The skeleton's a drone
and best ignored. Meanwhile, my hidden set
of struts and joists, stroll on. Forget. Forget.

Crooked Prayer

Please don't give me, Lord, the thing I covet:
silence silken as a candle flame,
or blank and pregnant as the moon
on which I might imagine any face
or none. Resist my wish
for cool white walls, windows flung open,
the afternoon hush edged with birdsong.
Give me again and again
this rattle of wind-spun trashcans,
the school bus with its screechy brakes,
two dogs poised at the sill to listen
and bay back their urgent wisdom.
Teach me to see unmade beds,
fruit torn into and abandoned,
pith and rind, as hungers
satisfied, to look in cracks
for what I step, unseeing, over:
rice grains, spilled beads, a lost needle, a burr,
and dust balls spun of nothing but nostalgia
of shed skin for a body, any body.

Perennial

You surprise me at noon.

We undress quickly,
meet under the faded blanket.
There's your familiar taste,

comforting as toast,
your skin's texture, soft lips
I'd know in utter darkness.

Your articulate tongue.

How many times
have we found each other
just like this? A homecoming.

Like the peonies that spill
from the earth each July—
the ornate layers

that fold inward, protective
of some luscious secret.

Around us, the house
holds its breath. The dogs
resign themselves to the rug.

So many days
we lose each other
in labyrinths of worry and work,

in detours so intricate
it seems we might never
find our way back

to this bed our bodies shaped.

APRIL LINDNER's first poetry collection, *Skin,* received the Walt MacDonald First Book Prize from Texas Tech University Press. Her novel, *Jane,* a modernization of *Jane Eyre,* was published by Poppy (Little, Brown) in 2010; *Catherine,* a modernization of *Wuthering Heights,* is forthcoming in 2013. A professor of English at Saint Joseph's University, April lives in Havertown, Pennsylvania, with her husband and sons.

Other Books from Able Muse Press

Michael Cantor, *Life in the Second Circle - Poems*

Catherine Chandler, *Lines of Flight - Poems*

Margaret Ann Griffiths, *Grasshopper - The Poetry of M A Griffiths*

Alexander Pepple (Editor), *Able Muse Anthology*

Alexander Pepple (Editor), *Able Muse - a review of poetry, prose & art*
(semiannual issues, Winter 2010 onward)

James Pollock, *Sailing to Babylon - Poems*

Aaron Poochigian, *The Cosmic Purr - Poems*

Matthew Buckley Smith, *Dirge for an Imaginary World - Poems*

Wendy Videlock, *Nevertheless - Poems*

Richard Wakefield, *A Vertical Mile - Poems*

www.ablemusepress.com

www.ingramcontent.com/pod-product-compliance
Lightning Source LLC
Chambersburg PA
CBHW021413090426
42742CB00009B/1125